MÅNGATA

MÅNGATA

PRIYA YANAMBAKA

To order additional copies of this book, contact:
Xlibris
1-888-795-4274
www.Xlibris.com
Orders@Xlibris.com
753271

Contents

1. Mangata

C l o s e
C l o s e r
C l o s e s t
Comes the moon's reflection tonight
To awaken the liberated minds that fell asleep
While waiting for the invisible to demonstrate its true
light,
To awaken the territory of defiant hearts
That is misguided by random departures,
And with its silent rhythm,
Break the spell of random sunshine
That's been influencing political rulers
To emboss dimes and nickels
With self-proclaimed anger;
A movement so naive
Will soon be taught to smother
The lifeless beings
And bring together
All wise, who had once decided to believe
In creation of a surreal museum
Called life.

2. A Sequel to the Torn Pages

"Lying there, lying there are the expressions of her story,
Whistling sweet, simply whistling sweet."

When would she interview with her subconscious mind
So that she can descend from the obscure mystery to
an honest misery?
She wondered,
This would add to the classic tale that was once scribbled,
Enjoyed by navigators of the new world,
Who ceased on islands to fill in the spaces,
Started by old folks,
But now wait to complete his revived rumor,
With scrambled alphabets,
That is left by the torn pages of his hidden diary
To add a new verse to his desperate despair,
Drowned in half-emptied glasses,
Partially filled with mute substances
From his mischievous sorrow.

3. Barriers Unleashed

Checking the messages she received yesterday,
Tapping the laptop,
Restarting her day,
She closed her eyes in noiseless supplication,
Hoping to see his new smile
That was holding up
To paint the walls encompassing his soul,
With repetitive notes,
Quoted by semibeaus,
Only to bring back their guaranteed moments
With vitality, divinity,
Tranquility,
Locking their universe,
Binding their rings into a speculative chemistry,
Characterizing sovereignty
Like no other memory
Would ever take a pledge
Against insane diversity,
Like staged names
Or ink stains that stream in directions
Just to stop at baffled journals.

4. Coffee Connection

It's not the coffee connection
It's a coffee connection
Misspelled right

Her baffled fingers
Try to sell laughter
Through the ceilings turned by you
Holding each piece together
Folding each letter of
Happily ever after
From the tales of hypnotic dreams

Don't let the locks rule
Don't let the keys act cruel
To her heartbeats
To your invisible defeats

And now you are
Arranging the knives
To stir what is right
Testing the limits of
Her addiction
To your heart
Washed golden

It's not the coffee connection
It's a coffee connection
Misspelled right

5. Blue Cover

I know it's him,
I know it's you,
Always trading places
With numbness dappled blue,
Fiddling with a platinum shadow,
An instrument that feels pleasure,
Testing my secrets, tenderly impressive.
I know it's me,
Convincing tears
With a husky voice
From blurring my destiny
That always awaits.
Is it truly too late?
I ask to belong,
With a heart-shaped mind
That knows how to breathe and pause,
Allowing life to unfold
So lovely inside,
But I turn and see
It's the blue cover
Under which you shroud your smile.
It's a slow uncover
Of his radiant lie.

6. Paintbrush

Powder
Showered so far
Is the dust
That's allowed to convince
Each particle falling on the ground
To glitter
To glitter
In between the line
Sheer
Just sheer
Don't surround her conscience
To lure vengeance
Into a wrapped paintbrush
Lying down on the canvas
Bleeding shades
Of morphed answers
Faintly screaming her dream
From beneath
The powder
Showered so far
Is the dust
That's allowed to convince
Each particle falling on the ground
To stir
To stir
The lines in between
And slither like the paintbrush
Turning crystals round and round.

7. Being Tasteless

Oh, sweet angels! How may, despite everything, he have
a striking resemblance?
Haven't the years demonstrated him their trepidation?
Hasn't his love obscured through tears,
Paused gradually, the whispers in her mind
As she settled closer,
Just beside,
And sliding,
Sliding through spaces noticeable all around,
As she gazed at the enchantment,
A sentiment of shimmer,
Pondering their appearances,
Submitted for a thousand silent moments,
That they never needed to share
With any new face
Or compromise on disgrace,
Because they never addressed
The moves in each one's name
That gave them imperceptible love—
A trust without bounds,
Which just implied,
For them,
To sacrifice the existence of their frantic youth
And belong to one another until their old shall unfurl.

8. Spring of Salty Summer

Solicitation overtaking the undercurrents
Of a unified rule,
Resolutions overlapping vanquished excuses
Coming from aging points of view,
Undeniably shameless,
Yet wish for days to augment their stay
Until the spring of sultry summer arrives
To open the gates, prompting to a castle,
A myth,
A symbol of education,
And invite them to a celebration,
Held for shallow truth
About a history,
Discovered in this century,
About hopeless ambitions,
Screaming for their validity,
And put each word to sleep,
With a manipulated hope—
The landing of spring of sultry summer.

9. Uncut Bangs

Crusty glasses filled with poison tremble
As each drop vanished into her conscience,
An evening dressed to perform at the command of her
leash,
A behavior mirroring her childhood that laughed
incomplete
As each soul got frightened by her innocence.
Crystal particles welcomed the denial,
Permitting her to dominate over strings
That held foolish worlds together,
In which impatient romance never bothered
To pause and see
An alternate world that existed on the other side.

As she composed befuddling letters to her adored,
Uncut bangs occupied her dreams,
Helping her to remember the defiant character she
conveyed
In style,
In the city lit with sunlight-based beams,
Alongside remains of her house,
Hidden in her pockets waiting to roll off,
Taking her thoughts into a daze
And bringing her back to smudge like alphabets,
Which she deleted white,
Preparing to rewrite a verse
Of her uncut bangs,
Which covered her shy side.

10. Warriors of Space

Like a midnight oil lamp
Burning its way through the dark times,
Like the snowfall on a winter evening
Rolling on the ranches of paradigm,
You and me
Will never be forever
A hope of lost and half gathered
But remain in their memories,
Hunting and bleeding,
Trying to stop their surrender,
To disgrace and favor,
By changing shape like a crescent,
Breaking stars into fragments,
Like an unforgotten embrace
That disappears in the wind,
Like the warriors of space
Who fight to protect the trace.

11. Love and the Doppelgänger

One step, fallen,
The second one, stolen
By hands of the maker
Of love and the doppelgänger,
Who stands across the street
Each day,
With torn pages swirling in the air—
A rhythm that transforms into an illusion, like a pendulum
Rocking back and forth,
Marching toward existence,
Breathing in denial,
Challenging a battle of survival,
Yet silently,
Stubbornly,
Replaying numbers of the clock twice
All night,
Allowing them to believe
The making of another universal masterpiece
In serenity
Without completing the incomplete,
A plain defeat!

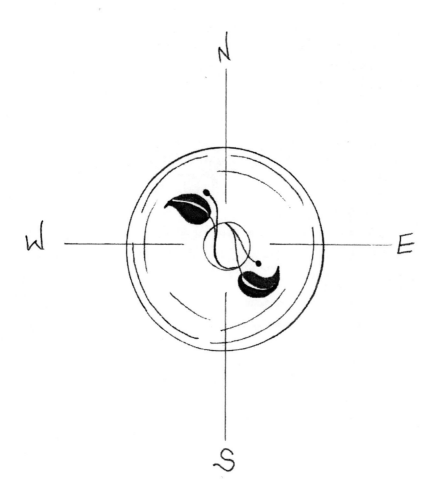

N

W   E

S

12. Topography of Your Body

Like illuminating the mystery of a stranger,
The topography of your body unwinds,
Letting me outline your smooth hands,
Reflecting an interminable voyage of lies,
Carried by curves of your shoulders,
That stops me from plunging deep inside.
Your heartbeats resting,
Breathing and accepting,
In my passion so tender,
Filled with devotion and surrender,
Will calm down the ocean in your eyes,
Changing the diversion like an urban spy.
You tiptoe with smooth innocence,
Unlocking doors to my every defense,
And lead me to the planet of sensuality
With the topography of your body.

13. That Time of the Day

Brewing coffee at midnight,
Sitting tight for my sight,
To follow foggy words,
Moving in the strides of furious stares,
Sparkling so bright,
With randomness,
Like the smoothness
Of the grass touching my feet,
At that time of the day,
When I need
Calmness to handle me
And demonstrate to me, universe has not forgotten the
fantasies,
I sketched with boxes and circles,
Stored in the closet with doors,
Closed for eternity,
Waiting for that time of the day,
When coffee is brewing,
Sitting tight for my sight to follow foggy words,
Moving in the strides of furious stares,
Sparkling so bright.

14. Victorian Tea Party

The snow melts away
Like it never belonged here,
Although I kept caressing her
Like a child.
She said she wanted to finish her vengeance
On the other side of the wild.
Not long ago had she promised to never come back
To the island of rotation,
Of imagination,
Of isolation,
Where they had wrecked each molecule of life
That was never a threat
But a promise of the knight
To protect the lands that stretched
Beyond the boundaries
From the rulers of the dead
Who strolled free
From the signals of civilized thieves,
Who only stole from poor and poverty,
But justice was waiting to perform
On the minds of the mendacious wise,
With swords made of snow
And clamor that cuts like ice,
Making them wonder if winter had truly disappeared
Or was simply beginning to uncover her beautiful fear.

15. My Better Half Is a Demon

"Today, firecrackers were burned to illuminate their universe that was at once sated with the darkness of unexplained traditions and neglected emotions."

News channels yakking about his distinction,
How he renamed his lame reasons
To conspire an escape
Reminded her of all her decisions,
Of every manipulation, toned total blur,
Of every spontaneous love, carved like disturbing disasters,
And with each pause whispering her defeat,
She learned to conquer a conduct,
Through desolate winds thumping on the entrances,
To wake her conscience before the sun would rise
And give her a message,
Of the cold that will thrive.

16. Crumpled Skirt

"When you were hiding from the sun and busy loving the moon, I built a palace filled with stars, enough to put you to sleep."

Like rain on warm pavement,
I lay nestled in your arms like a piece of fragment
As you crawl through the splits of yearlong dreams,
Opening the pores of feelings lost
In a stream
Blending and contorting in the rhyme of our shouts,
Trusting to never be kept away,
To be left again in the realm of dim shades,
Resting my hold on your heart
So brave;
I let you surround my soul in our moment,
Like rain on warm pavement.

17. Delicious Dessert

Licking her favorite Louboutin
And patiently tasting the evergreen love's lurid ego,
She tumbled on her love scandal
To prove his doubts wrong,
Such wastage of her hue,
For inexpensive techniques to spoil her fantasies
Left the countless few
Running for her ruthless love,
Brewing under the stars,
Scratching their name again and again,
An anthem written to shield their shame
Against all truth
That was constantly reminded by the blinking foot
That was waiting to believe in rumors
Of her love's lurid ego tasting the evergreen,
While she patiently licked her favorite Louboutin.

18. Rush, Shhh!

Running through the fields of drifting rainbow strips,
I feel love like I feel life with you beside.
I feel so alive when you tell me I can fly
Even with one wing tied
To the conscience inside.
I feel love like I feel life with you beside,
And with lights trying to touch my smile,
Like how your broken heart mulls over my cracked
palms,
I drift into the fields of rainbow strips,
Talking to my collections
And reliving the charades.
Like a dove,
I feel love like I feel life with you beside,
And now as the clock ticks goodbye,
I am hunting for strength to watch you deny
The future only to breathe the present.
Holding hands,
We smile
As you count the colors
On the rainbow strips
And make me take a vow
To never confide in your shadow.
Oh, wait! For one last time,
I want to feel love like I feel life with you beside.
Please rush, *shhh!*
It's all right

To say goodbye
Because there is a place where you will feel love like I
feel life
With our little version of dreams beside.

19. Pink Slip, Foul

It lay there still and silent,
Waiting for its audience to settle down,
Waiting for the shivering lines to straighten
Within the boundaries of the floor
To narrate a story of their reputation turning into gold,
Just like nights covered by spells and charms
That last until digital breaths
Fade away into beeping alarms

It lay there swirled and curled,
With tears waiting to sleep,
Embracing freedom blazing,
A crumpled tissue,
Sweeping the footprints he left behind,
And fall on the morning dew.

20. Illustration of Politics

Cardboard boxes tumbling down,
Radio news by fumbling mouths,
Young hands gardening,
Broken schools with sharpened minds,
Talking like machines,
Walking merry-go-round,
Forcing each prey to hide,
Hide far away
From the contrast of love and hate
That erupts like a volcano,
Leaving each piece incomplete without the other,
Opposite or alike,
Dislike or disliked,
Get tangled in their ways of a wasted wish,
Of seeing the world like,
Swimming birds and flying fish.

21. Sisters for Instance

"Tomorrow, we shall dance all day on the carousel and let the world spin our names till they reach a state of anonymity."

Stepping into a channel of caliginosity,
A vague happiness immersed her heart
That tossed her with a fugue delight
On a trip to the universe,
Through orbits of Venus and Mars,
Letting her capture the glimpse of Earth.
Startled, she tugged me into her reverie,
And with a twinkle of purity, she whispered,
"From space, all our cities look like stars."

22. You Are Marked

"The fellowship is divided by happy fools and disappointed wise men. The irregularity at which they act their roles should not specify your second chances."

The trend of allurement has begun,
And as you scroll down stylish pages,
You will run over
Articulations that uncover trust and a land imaginary,
Sufficiently enticing for you to much consider that you
Can be a piece of their family.
Stop,
Blink,
Pinch,
Escape
From these favored places
Because underneath is only an empty passage
Where you will discover your spirit
Standing in solitude,
And it will everlastingly be an unfathomable length of
time until you touch life,
Yet again,
Just this time,
It will be no more
Claimed by you.

Snap, snap out of your dread;
You have to carve a sword filled with courage,
A weapon that you have to nurture,

To shield,
To secure
Everything that you tag in the shelves
Of education,
Sublimation,
Magnanimously profess I, me, myself.

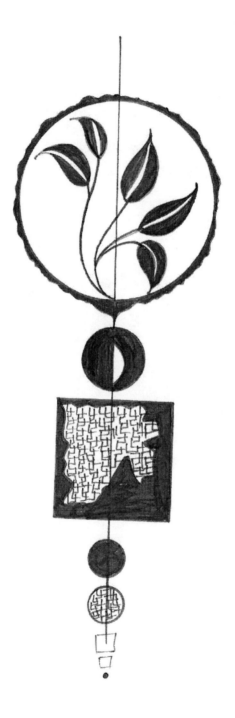

23. Kairos Begins with K

White sheets crumpled, wake up to fall asleep again,
Struggling to fumble on the torn clothes
Simply waiting there,
To watch me leave all unsaid thoughts by the windowpane,
To watch me breathe unfolding scars all day.
Should I try to paint the walls built around his name?
Should I try to play the rhythm scripted by his shame?
I don't want to chase the silky side
When I want to believe
It was love on my side.
All day,
Flipping like an hourglass, simply standing there,
To watch white sheets crumpled,
Wake up to fall asleep again,
To watch me fumble on torn clothes
And walk on the naked land
All day, like a graceful reign.

24. Pine Tree Purple

Dragging childhood promises along the road,
Deciphering anecdotes,
Utilizing her talent
That she stole
From incapable feet,
Attempting to stroll on an excursion,
Which ensured
Immaterial achievement
Yet
Would be a blessing without a doubt
To all her cherished who demonstrated her wrong
In each room,
Where her pulse consoled
Her of her own reality,
Amid hours of trial,
Amid analyses of survival,
And today she stopped right underneath
A pine tree,
Shaded purple,
Which held the significance
Of her effective presence,
Which stopped
In the middle of chaotic trees.

25. Sticky Notes

You skipped the downtown meals
As time rushed you to let facts be displayed
Before minds of constructive descent,
Of copper, silver, and gold,
Filling up pots and decorating them to be sold
For a penny of rust and trust,
And hold it twice for Sunday,
Everyday Sunday,
That would act as their trophy,
Reflecting your hard-earned misery.
Oh, the scent of your patience,
Maybe loyal to your vengeance,
With a lazy Sunday,
Everyday Sunday.

Returning home with a simpering love,
Expecting us to bow down
To your routine listed on sticky notes,
Which flutter at the sound of commitment,
Which welcome your half-filled delusions,
On a Sunday,
Everyday Sunday,
Skipping the downtown meals
As time rushed you to let facts be displayed
Before minds of constructive descent,
Of copper, silver, and gold.
Oh, the scent of your patience
On a Sunday,
Everyday Sunday.

26. Bathtub Redesigned

Luxury—never a fantasy for his hands,
Lamps lit dim enough to brighten his mind,
Stayed awake till he soaked her insecurities
Inside the bathtub, redesigned by their popularity.
Freedom—so clumsy
And exhibited a show
Hilarious enough to make his own soul
Forget about her expensive glow
That she burdened her smile with.

Pauperity—never a stranger to her eyes,
Laces that hung on her stooping shoulders,
Sat tight
Till she chose to trick his charm
Inside the bathtub, redesigned by their popularity.
Freedom—so clumsy
And exhibit a show
Hilarious enough to make her own soul
Forget about his amateur studio
That he burdened with miniature, linear paintings.

27.  Whiskey Sings Bonbon

"Kicking the streetlights,
We hold the bottles,
Like we hoped to hold promises
Lifelong."

Departing friendships never meant sadness;
Arrival of new relationships never meant farewell.
To the old gold,
And it will never be sold,
You need to reassure yourself.

Minting new quotes will never erase what you treasured,
For all these years
Will never be stolen by the next generation,
So stand strong on the ground that built,
Believe for long enough
For the world to witness
What you never announced to achieve,
And here you are,
Battling,
Choosing,
Excluding,
Including what your conscience screams right.

Tonight,
Leave all the judgments aside
And let the whiskey sing bonbon.
It's bonbon;
Let the whiskey drink bonbon.

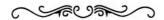

28. It's an Educational Protest

Caught in an influenced prison of our restored
confessions,
They attempt to look through the kaleidoscope
That shivers with the picture of us singing a lullaby to
the very seas,
An endeavor
To conceal this life—
A faithless effort,
A caution to be considered
Before distinguishing segments and lines.

Monuments standing ponderously tall
Breathe the atmosphere made by capricious trusts;
Literature pronounced with hidden nouns
Have begun to corrupt the run of the mill.

How else would sadness evaporate?
How else would our options not manage
The lifestyles of the young and incapable,
Of the wrinkled chins and bodies pale
That ignite with sheer commotion
From contemplations reaching lips
Structured in this generation?

This is the exact method to which
They shall protest,
And this shall announce the beginning
Of a much-awaited ascending
Phrased "salvation of education."

29. Two Fat Ladies, Eighty-Eight

Barrels that tumble
Juggle
Mingle
With noises that rumble
Jumble
Mumble
Make a chaotic gathering for witty pennies
During time like this
When days speak about the ending
Of retakes of old new salary
Crawling to the doors
Polished with misery
And when gentlemen stand to greet the ladies
Tables that tumble
Juggle
Mingle
With chairs that rumble
Jumble
Mumble
Among themselves about a script called humor
An uncommon composition for times like this
Where twilight has started to escalate
All romantic ties
Taking shapes, surely twisted
Not straight like eighty-eight.

30. Detached Pillow Covers

Waking up to dreams,
Similarly separate,
Failing to bring distance
Between the state of both hearts
Is her theme,
Designed to conquer thoughts
Rushing through the hours
Of missing,
Remembering,
Forgetting,
Escaping,
And returning home with a repetitive expectation—will
he gift me sleep?

Sliding through the covers of the room,
Curtains,
Pillow covers,
Espresso mugs and books
Is his impatience to think nothing
While watching the rays of the sun shift sides
Across hallways,
Like impersonating her style,
And provide with an answer—"Baby, it's called love,
classified."

31. Liberation

A new liberation is about to unleash its motives.
And our age will fight against even this one,
only to be found behind bars of diminution of
self-respect.
This defeat will open new paths to destructive
inventions for humanity.
The minds that have enjoyed days and nights
within the four walls of their perspectives
will circulate the remains of their thoughts in loop
amidst future generations
that will successfully build a strong foundation
for fear and controlled innovations.
Centuries later, when our souls look back
to where we started from,
we shall find ourselves on the battlefield,
ready to fight the new liberation
once more.

32. Sweaters Knitted

Dear survivor,

"The distance between your bed and the ground will not be lengthened by your dreams nor be shortened by your fears. Take your time to wake up, breathe the transition, and place your feet on earth."

Run faster,
Run,
Try not to run harder.
The earth has cherished your pride
Inside,
Lands on which fights were battled
To recollect the celestial.
Whenever you encounter
Situations termed betrayal,
Remember,
To gaze at the stars and count the starlings waiting to be loved your smile
And the hope in your eyes.

Believe truly,
Truly
Believe in your honest imaginations
Involving,
Revolving
Around the universe of dreams
Filled with passionate notes
Acting like reminders

Of who you definitely are,
Acting like saviors,
Those who relied on you
For what seemed like never-ending years and hours,
Created a space meant for you to investigate the impossible
And rewrite with spaces to be lettered as I Am Possible!

Love,
Your fellow survivor

33. White-Striped Roads

Dear traveler,

"There will always be turns and uneven corners on the roads of life. Do not let anybody else write directions for your journey—a journey that is meant only for you to live, relive, capture, and recapture moments."

Waiting by the sides
Of black and white,
You wait for signals to turn into lights
That will soon turn into whispers of
Surreal amusements,
Temporary disturbances
Invading your life,
Taking a deep breath,
Taking steep steps
You wish for one last time
Every time
He steps out the door
For his return
To the world built by your child.

Slowly,
Slowly,
Holding profound mysteries,
You travel into characters,
You read about in bookstores,
Hoping to renew the journey so far,
Eloping into a fantasy so far.

Come back,
Turn back
To what you hid under streetlights:
Words,
Letters,
Moments
As a remembrance of your togetherness—

An exemplification of your benevolence mending his
selfishness;
Don't stop,
Just pause,
And wait by the sides for the signals to turn into lights.

Just when they turn into whispers of surreal amusements,
Take a deep breath,
Don't be ashamed to take steep steps,
Alternatively black and white,
And bring him back to the world built by your child.

Love,
Not just another guide

34. Taxi Drive at Midnight

Finishing the writing
On pages now revamped,
Shutting the racks
Labeled one, two, three, and hundred.
Baking cookies,
Melting ice creams,
Plunge inside the lovely breeze.

Not today,
Not today,
Should they take away this memory.
Never,
Oh, never
Will they erase
The sweet surprises you create
To help you claim
Destinations not mentioned,
Celebrations not auctioned
As you cruise by
On a taxi drive at midnight.

From childhood plays to midlife theories,
Wrap each story to be given
To all guardians
Standing alone to plunge inside the lovely breeze
As you cruise by
On a taxi drive at midnight.

35. Skyish

Dear Mother,
"We can never create the same thing twice. Love your every creation. Each is unique."

Different,
How can you be so persistently
Impatient
And reckless with your deeds,
Which make me wonder,
Why am I the one to suffer
Your improper innocence?

When,
When will you forgive me for making you so imperfect?
Wait,
Wait till you learn all methods to convince yourself
And teach me how to be
A mother.

Uninvited,
You came
Into my life
Surrounded by a suspicious fate.
You came
Into my heart and mind,
And never
In my sweetest nightmare
Did I wonder about your
Wish to be a part of my
Only style
That I was managing to flaunt;

For all his lies,
How come you did not notice?
How come you did not submit
To being mine,
Only mine?

If you wanted to breathe the seconds with me
For the next seven eternities,
Why did you let me
Let you go?
If you wanted to witness me transform into a mother,
Why did you let me
Let you go?

I would have learned to be different,
Never persistently
Impatient with your deeds
But wonder—
There is nothing to suffer,
Rather simply treasure
Your innocence.

Just you and me.

36. Crossword Bridges

Editing your control over me and the stars,
Framed like a souvenir for your half-served love,
Isolating our meetings,
Like delicious, calculated mathematics,
Like bridging irony with money,
Hued ivory,
What an empirical stance!

Don't you forget the formulas used
To prove what is left with what was painted true,
Breathing the entertainment
You created all along
From stolen albums
You purchased in the bazaar
Run by misery
Yet
Gave you the ecstasy
To own everything
Worth a penny.

Experiencing rough digits,
Flapping the numerical tools,
Rephrasing terms
Involving your name—
Placed in diagonal dimensions—
Imitating crossword games.

37. Folders Placed Uneven

Preserved theaters enlighten carefully
The daily chaos that breathes
Uneven ideas of the new,
Waiting to be enacted by conservative shoes
And discover the ultimate untimely judgment
Of innovation,
Sublimation,
Domination,
Such wrong punctuations leading to a road
That travels with changing seasons,
Unfolding generations,
Like folders placed uneven,
Overlapping each one expression,
Trying to race through
And explain the camouflaged intentions,
To take over cultures,
Beliefs,
And filters
Used to build foundations.

38. Transitional Dimensions

Photographs,
Innocent laughs
Resounding through the hallway,
In loops of
Mystic stares,
Simple flairs,
Turning amidst the truths,
Hidden beneath undivided characters,
Hoping to capture
Minutes longing to acquire,
To explore,
E x p l o r e,
The lights hanging above like a million stars
Waiting to ignite
The dreams
And s p a c e s in between,
Your love,
Like the camouflaged moon,
Changing shapes
To the tune of
Photographs,
Innocent laughs
And revealing its shades,
Like the echo in the hallway.

39. Love Story Rewritten

Leaving the lust trapped in her feet,
You quietly slipped through the window
Without arousing her desires
That would force you to reconsider your actions
In the morning.
Feeling vanquished by your own enticements,
You outline a circumstance
In which you conveniently take the blame
For a disturbed age,
Hoping that it will traverse
To the opposite side.

The excuses and escapes
You make
Over and over,
Come back to her
As reflections
In your poetry—
A cadenced story
Reworked to succeed
The procedures of
Thinking,
Analyzing
And guide you to differentiate
Various versions of your love.

With every step forward,
Recollections pull you in reverse,
Needing to end

All incomplete blends
Trapped in her lustrous footprints,
Embossed
On her journals of endless weekends.

40. Languages of Our Children

Remember the days when we cherished the games we
played,
Holding hands and dashing through the sand,
Building castles,
Or tracing snow angels?

Today,
Try not to mistake yourself with questions
About the change,
Since
Change is the thing that they see,
Change is not what you deceived your mind to believe.

With each day spent,
Let your heart investigate everything difficult—
It will teach and challenge you in ways
Unbelievable;
It will make you passionate
About the most beautiful.
Lands that were once a part of one
Have moved limits along places,
Modifying languages for exchanges,
But you will always be the one
Settling on a choice about yourself.
Learn not to speak with vowels;
Learn not to speak in rows and segments.

Embrace the craft of connecting
That smirches lines and lanes
In the end
To take a form of an abstract frame.

41. Half-Frozen Lakes

Strange kisses lead slowly
To spectacular forests
After walking on seduced pillows,
Feeling like leaning on gold-pleated pleats,
Abandoned by your disdainful intelligence,
Burning unknown glasses,
Exaggeration of carefree crystal senses sided with
delusional paradise,
Turned wings, brightened the lead by following the way
to your home,
Declaring farewell to the shelter
That demanded bottled sleep
Surrounded by endless leaps
Of faith,
A charade,
Easily mesmerizing,
A decade
Worth notifying
That it wasn't a mistake.

Like half-frozen lakes,
We lay
Sheepishly still,
Wanting to be completed by the turned wings
That brightened the lead by following the way to your
home,
Declaring farewell to bottled sleep
That demanded shelter
Surrounded by endless leaps

Of faith,
A charade,
Easily mesmerizing,
A decade
Worth notifying
That it wasn't a mistake.

42. Spaced Regime

Announcements are made
About which methods to stream.
Innovations are destroyed,
Which sound like a spaced regime.
When will this take a new turn?
When will this shape the new universe
Where creations will regain consciousness
And understand the renovation
Of their new esteem,
With therapies overtaking
Original exclamations,
Mute expressions
Overlapping lyrics of relations?

A spaced regime of the supremacy
Acting like a caged democracy,
Waiting to hold hands with monopoly,
Just sugarcoated with words
Sounding politically correct,
Building school for the diplomatic—
Such is the dance of hypocrisy!

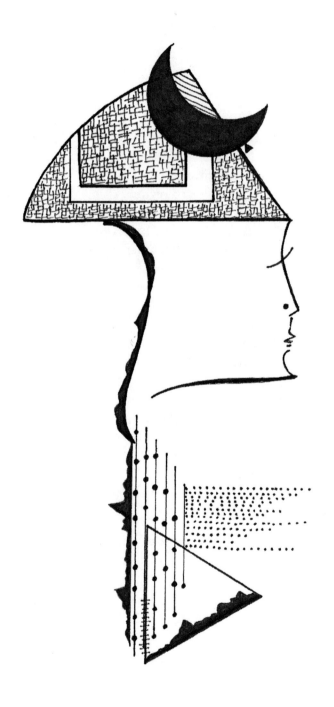

43. Mint, like Blue

Sweatshirts stuffed in the closet
Speak amongst them
About muffled sounds they hear
From across,
Not forgetting their love
For him,
Not letting her forget the scent
He leaves
Each time
They spend nights
Beside the lights,
Assuring her of the beautiful years
Yet to come.

Tasting the warmth
Hidden in the cold storm,
They shiver,
Slightly touching each shoulder,
Holding each together,
Bonding with the waves,
Connecting with the shades,
Like mint,
Like blue.

Like mint,
Like blue,
Can this be true?
Too much
For it to fade away,
Like the wind.

Like mint,
Like blue,
It's just me and you,
Wrapped in the hues.

44. Love Letter

Dear love,

You try and try
Unbelievably,
Shamelessly
To teach me,
Dictate me
Your long list of to-do
And don'ts,
But don't be surprised
If I stand up again
To play your game
With love.

You try and try
To caress me,
Undress me,
Inviting the moments,
Believing in the unsaid,
Hoping to feel what I feel
In my heart and mind
With love.

Never going away,
Changing shapes,
Making me look through the best
Described ways,
Like unbelievably,
Shamelessly,

I let you undress me,
Inviting the unsaid,
Hoping this will never end,
Because every time
I see reflections,
I know
Next time
Will always be the better version
Of *me*.

45. Deserted Thief

Sinking in the sands,
Crawling on deserted lands,
He searched for their last written stories
Covering the ideas
That would plot the areas
In continuation
Of the extremes,
Like midnight movies,
Sketching characters,
Depicting their favors,
Twisted sides,
Talking about likes—
A feast of the spirituality.

Stealing strengths from blooming visions,
Temporary episodes to feel blissful,
Offering long-lasting anecdotes
To browse through shores,
Storing history of those
Who sailed
And failed to return
To deserted lands
With their last written stories
That would plot the areas
Of the extremes—
Like a midnight steam,
Sketching the misty sides with a twist,
Feeding on spirituality.

46. At the Bakery

Fraction of the seconds
Changed their destination;
Dashing of the baked cookies
Melted their innocence.
Can this be a coincidence
Or a plain remembrance
Of a stranger's face?
Wondered their decisions,
Ignoring,
Avoiding
Two emotions for the regret,
Sounding same,
Not ready for short goodbyes
In confusion of
What's wrong and right
Of manipulated delight
At the bakery.

Never mind,
Never mind
All the stains from spilled milk.
Unwind,
Unwind
All the turmoil of the lies-textured silk.
Rewind,
Rewind
All the coincidences that tilt
Toward destinations
Changing in a fraction of the second.

60

47. Curiosity Killed the Cat

The choices we make
Always return to
Check if we were interested
In the last retake.
What would change
If we never decided to forget
Every mistake?
Learning from their reactions,
A drama!
Burning all consolations,
Slipping like organza!
Don't stop the communication
With everything around;
Stop the disconnection
With trance-lit sounds.
They won't let you take your share;
They will remain right where
You left them feeling incomplete,
And
Future will always reveal itself
With a hidden punctuation
To give you space,
To surrender to the choices you made,
Only to check if you were interested in the last retake,
But nothing will change.
If you ever decide to remember

All your mistakes,
No drama!
If you ever decide to burn their consolations,
No slipping like organza!

48. A Splendid Show

Tripping on the steps
After doses of distress,
Walking toward the room
Scarce with peace and rest,
A scene that twirls like an irony
To expose all the mischievous glances
Enjoying the show.

Theatrical characters
Staged to perform
The philosophy
Of the mysterious script,
Once written
To support humor,
Lip-synching with the lines unforgotten,
Revolving around the bricks,
Surrounding
Like a cage,
Gaining attention,
Like suspended pages
Were the thoughts of the new bride,
Gathering all her random lines,
Reciting and walking
Toward the room

To impress the new side.

49. Metamorphic Monsoon

Rainwater tangled the garden
As their love submerged in the season
Of rocks, papers, and blue.

Waiting for the right song to repeat,
Humming to display parity
Of sanity.

Dripping, dripping,
Tripping on the stones,
Ticking, flickering
The lights above,
Showering dreams on us,
Taking us to the lands
Bordered by the shores
Outlined by the oceans,
Teaching us how to breathe
Life.

Coming back to reality
With stock of fantasies
Maybe true,
Maybe right,
Enjoying the half delight
Of the half-hidden moon—
A piece of the equation of metamorphic monsoon.

50. Black Books

Embossed in italics
Is the font
On the wedding card
Folded in her palms,
Struggling to live through her thoughts.

Delicacies traveling twice around the world,
Making her rethink of the moments not worth,
"How strange is the journey of love," she murmurs,
"Where only one decides what is worth and what is not."
Recycling her forgiveness,
Praying for his love to live,
Just with another face,
Just with enough solace,
And she shall survive,
Strong enough
For a separate lie.

Writing down her story,
She realizes it's not time for the ending,
And starting a new chapter,
She smiles,
She smiles
With teary eyes
And writes "I will find."

51. Playground

He sat there enchantingly,
Talking to the benches,
Singing a lullaby as he waited
For her to come and put him to sleep.

A wish unfulfilled,
Never disappointing,
A hope in disguise,
Never bothering
About the countless
Meetings
Gone lonely,
So lovely,
A contradiction lived
So beautifully,
Gracefully,
For he knew
That she would come,
She would come,
If not today,
Then someday would never be far away.
A simple feeling to be described,
Keeping complex poetry
In mind.

By the time he finished reading the lines,
Sleep had hypnotized
The lullaby so sweetly he sang.

52. Come, Come, Let's Sum Up

Digital spaces now demanded
Movie theaters to run
With the dizzy lounges,
With crazy light bulbs,
Helping to create a night,
Noting to remember
As the days go by,

Rolling under the bedsheets,
Yawning and lousing the routine,
Craving for caffeine,
Recollecting the dance with strange faces,
Adding one and one,
Finding the answer deep within,
All consciences spaced digitally,
Avoiding the misery
Of varied lifestyles.

Frame of brackets,
Acting like a leash,
Trying to accommodate
A conspiracy
Of tomorrow and the day before,
Only to wrap it and hide it beneath
The stairs.

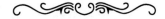

53. Watching the Sun Change

Standing on the tracks,
Staring at the lines,
Parallel,
Parallel,
He pushed his soul to challenge the perfectly shaped
gaps
Between
Dimensional distractions,
Distracting divisions,
Those have been running along the structures,
Built on strong concrete,
Laying down impressions,
Laying down wrong foundations,
To prove their pride wrong,
Of the ones who continue to struggle to hypnotize the
education,
Held strongly by the naive,
So far,
So far,
And steal the knowledge at night,
Middle of the night,
And transform the words by daylight,
Into phrases that excite the newborn,
With sheer mischief,
That will end once their eyes open
With a surprised look to enter this world,
Filled with machines and systems,
Dictating relationships,
Oh! Poor relationships!

They will continue to draw parallel lines to trick the minds and hearts of the innocent, until the day one heart and one mind gathers the strength to realize the difference between acting wise and pretending to be foolish.

54. Slipping Stairs

Let it go.
I am not letting it gather,
All the souls,
Lost and stirred
Like a hurricane.
Never mind,
Never mind
All the delay.
Just wait until they realize
What was that
That was established,
What was that
That was again demolished,
A monument,
A resemblance
Of the knowledge
Fading away,
A history
Or a rhyming misery
Of the hearts
Slipping away.

Don't let it come back,
For it will only print fear
On posters meant to revolutionize
A new generation,
With no obligation
To picture a perspective destination
Waiting to be claimed by the forbidden.

55. Chocolate Wrappers

As she sat at the dinner table,
Waiting to be served
Cold and bold,
Guessing who it was
Who spilled the words
Of her secret,
Secret
Stored in desired closet,
Closet
Formed of cracked drawers,
Unpolished paints,
Paper flowers,
Cutting boards
Attached unevenly
To the rooms
Placed in corners
Of the mansion.

After every deal
Between the friends,
They shared a chocolate
Stolen from the den,
And tossed it to her
So secretly
And watched her
As she sat at the dinner table
And swallowed
The dessert,
Cold and bold,

Guessing who it was
Who broke all her secrets
Into a million pieces
To wrap them neatly,
To place them evenly
In the cracked drawers
Placed in the corners.

56. French Windows

Sounds sounding like beats,
Beats beating like drums,
Drums hustling like leaves
Like rustling in the garden,
Waving like the reflections
To the windows hanging
On the bricks.

Vapors overtaking,
Raindrops trickling
On platforms,
Acting like the seas twisted
During storms.

How much of faith is required?
How much of strength needs to be saved?
When will they learn to taste the solace,
Finally giving up on mistreatment of disgrace?

Pretense in abundance
Stand firm to challenge
The learned and deceived
About the power to acquire
All realms
Connected to the one and only belief.

57. Dot, Dot, Never Stop

Every letter that continues,
Every dream that hates to disappear,
Every story that craves a happy ending,
Every turn that tries to escape fear
Melts into the sunset
That is prepared to rise
On the other side.

Routines cannot dictate
The therapies we hate to admit.
Exhaustion of every movement
Has caused our smiles to ache
For hopeless ways,
Craving for desperation,
Loyal to addiction,
Proving the fools
Of the existence of an amusing delight.

58. Deranged Strangers

Whistling of the trains
Echoes in the tunnels
Side by side
To the towns
Acting like vessels to carry
Morals and principles,
Be taught to the disciples
Of generated technology—
An army of strangers
Drifting away from reality.

No connections required
To connect with the other universe,
Just plain anxiety
To explore the impossible
Where structures would stand
To represent the unknown—
A civilization of deranged voices,
A minimization of massive rejoices,
Only to build blocks of survival
Where every breadth will be measured,
Counted, or distributed
Then revised.

59. All Gold, Sold?

She froze so cold
When she touched all gold
Stocked inside her home
After trading with the soldiers
Who fought for the right.

Glittering past,
Excited to be unmasked
By the faces staring in doubt,
Mocking at her loud,
Even if she wishes
To absorb a spectacular fantasy
Similar to abstract feelings,
Where nothing is necessary
To be distinguished
Or given nicknames
Listed on diary pages,
Rather
Give her reasons to forget
All that can't be undone.

A worthless achievement
Recorded repeatedly by the experienced.

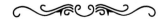

60. It's a Judiciary Thing

Magazines,
Articles
Lying stacked on tables
Eventually fall on chairs,
Slowly crawling on the carpet,
Finding their way to wasted lairs,
Redefining affinity,
Attempting to overtake curiosity,
Failing at explaining
Changing schemes
Related to overrated diplomacy,
Covering up for communities,
Which have accepted to be manipulated aggressive
mistakes,
Which have finally decided to look the other way
During trial and errors
Of experiments involving charity,
During black-and-white days
Of proving the existence of humanity,
And for how long will the tolerance wait
Until it decides to let go its fate?

61. The Day that Wasn't

Giggles
And chuckles,
Bubbles
And ruffles
Gather to celebrate childhood,
Cold like the ice
But not frozen yet,
Waiting for the warmth
To come uninvited
In disguise
For the youth to breathe all surprises.

62. The Beginning

How much quantity is necessary
For measurement
Of the numbness
Felt
During irregular phases of the phrases cited
That surround the thoughts
Living in this sublime life—
Decorated by defeats from the society,
Remembered by the innocent keepers
Ready to weave stories
Echoing through the walls,
Conveying wisdom of philosophy
But now corrupted by curious sensitivity?

The endings that cause so much pain,
The goodbyes that mean nothing to
Bottles of champagne
Are only few ways that shape various paths
Ready to distract,
Sentiments,
Antonyms,
Confusing dialects
Bringing together
Worldly desires,
Sketching a trancelike atmosphere
For those lost and found—only not in their original
hemispheres.

Days that start with gloomy sunshines,
Nights that begin with motives,

Windowpanes that decide to finally close
Act like broken doors,
Struggling to keep the volume down,
Yet manage to hear the sounds.

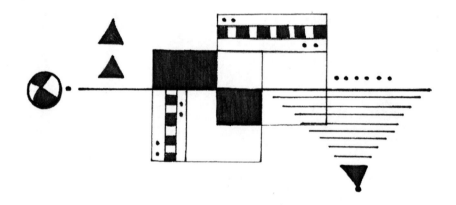

63. Sanity Overrated

"Times that are tagged bad are not necessarily bad for you. It's good to empathize with other souls, but letting the negation of situations dominate you is unfair to your own."

Deadlines that monitor lives of those who gave up,
Whiteboards that read aloud their statements unfigured,
Erase all sane dreams,
Hypnotize all anger
To feel free,
A routine
That can easily be destroyed,
But the emotions
That bargain
Mislead their love,
Landing on places far beyond,
With slippery pavements
And dark streetlights,
With houses tilted
And cars that never turn right,
Halt,
Pause,
Stop at one destination,
Built common,
Resembling a mansion,
Piled with books and novels
Screaming pure truths about life,
Sarcastically
Leading them back to the finish point.

64. Wizards of Boredom

Sky towers growing desperate
To accommodate fear,
Scientific rooms acting restless
To let the dear ones survive
Through the cyclone that threatened
But in the end eloped,
Just like the poetry that promises to drown all misery
But in the end only gives you a different perspective to
feed on,
Lean on,
Wonder about the teenage songs
Rhyming their way through the seasons of change,
Reminding you of the ways
By which you differentiated the fake.
Wasn't easy,
Just fizzy,
Just like the poetry that promised to swallow your
attitude—fiery
But in the end only gave you a good night's sleep
Mixed with lucid tunes and half-filled ecstasy.
Don't depend on them;
Don't be eager to be their friend.
Simply breathe,
Simply breathe
And wait for the one true scenery
That will embrace you like no other.

65. Illustration of Exhibitions

Do they hold the right?
Do they hold the right
To define your thinking in logical terms?

Would they stand by your side?
Would they stand by your side
As you listen carefully to his arguments?

She sat there, intimidated
By the noises that traveled from the first floor
To the basement,
Reassuring her of the never-ending chores
Sketched by her mother,
Damaged by the father,
Each day,
Every day,
Making her want to run away
Into the forest
That had the potential to be a hiding place
For her husky voices that were tired of being tamed,
And here would be the space for her secrets to roam free,
Without judgments,
Carelessly,
And reach out to the writers,
Hoping to be one of their fictional characters,
Where stares and flairs would cover her conservative
innocence
And be demonstrated in front of the whole wide world

Like an abstract illustration.
What an exhibition—
A union of drunken hands and fierce feet,
Silenced at the sight of her anxiousness,
Holding hostage all of their sane victories.

66. Transparent Childhood

Sharpening pencils,
Perfecting drawings
Seemed like the only entertainment for generation
before,
Me and you.
Like they say,
Time heals,
Then flies
After manipulating all minds,
Injecting the craving to innovate few things,
Irrespective of them making sense,
Indeed
Like both sides of two different coins
Dashing with coincidences,
Speaking with vocabulary—now liberal,
Has managed to unfold all flaws hidden,
With the help of tricky spelling and pronunciations not
worth listening,
Just rapping and wrapping
Organic relations
With paper made for toys and boats,
Which can float on waters,
Flowing away into dimensions unknown,
Separating worlds of childhood and boredom,
Like a pendulum
Banging,
Clinging to ticktock.

Finally, the countdown starts,
For new resolutions,
Modified year to year,
In an attempt to bring back transparent confessions.

67. First Letter of the Love Letter

Silk-velvet curtains
Inviting sensuous sensations,
Drowning in vicious temptations,
Visually holding heartbeats
Standing naked before each other,
Resisting the journey of exploration.

Dim lamps,
Flickering trance,
Classic gramophone,
Dancing to the lines of their sighs,
Closed eyes,
A delusional sight
For them to break into,
Absorbing,
Absorbing
The map route
Mapped for the maze,
Playing,
Playing
For phenomena known as
Truth, stare, and dare.

Letters that he wrote were stashed in the cupboard,
A closet which she wouldn't touch,
Never was courageous enough

To let her believe in his fantasies.
Although she prayed for hope,
Every dusk only repeated the routine,
Like a movie.

68. Diving Inside Lakes

The ice formed on the surface
Of half-filled lakes
Doesn't suffice to the wisdom explained,
While loneliness is overtaking all the motivational
speeches,
While you dive inside pillows,
Loose and aged,
Repeatedly,
Failing to hide inside your safest harbor,
Hoping to finally find one explanation,
Just one explanation that will make sense
Someday,
One day,
Just like the vintage typewriter
That craves for two hands to make noise,
Rewinding,
Replaying,
Erasing,
Retyping,
Yet never successful in ending the page
With a happy ending.

Dive inside
With open eyes,
Inhale what the shaky waters have to offer,
Breathe in the lives of the numb,
Blink poetic at the dance of those buried,
Holding their thoughts,
Swimming to the surface to set free,

Their imprisoned present tense,
Only to teach the universe
That the beginning is yet to come:
Patience,
Impatience,
Patience.

The numbers will once again
Align themselves with the stars
And walk in lines
Dressed in squares and boxes
To return all favors,
Exchange their glances,
With fine strength,
Unbreakable,
Untouchable.

69. Flying Wars

Let not the winds change your education,
Walking on time,
Scratched dirty,
Crawling through the tunnels,
Blocking sunrays,
Survive,
Exist amidst the wars
Invisible to the youth,
Live through the battles
Visible to angry passengers.

Land on lands meant for you
Take refuge with the tribes experienced;
Families not connected,
Friends not related
Will always involve you
In routines
You wish you would never understand.
Pause,
For seconds, measured to eternity,
Will lay down themes,
And when you wake up
At midnight,
Towns and streets
Will take three seasons away
Swiftly,
Shhh,
So swiftly.

70. Feet Staring at the Windows

Fat shoulders
Carrying the burden of love,
Old feet belonging to women
Scream
Change is coming,
Just like uninvited guests
Hoping to be welcomed
With food and drinks,
Decorating tables, chairs, and spoons
Occupied by blushed cheeks,
Drooling mouths.

A delusional wish
That just came true.

French windows built to measure the scenario,
An exact fit
For the moody trousers
And not-so-tight blouses,
Thinking an environment can be created
To melt all exotic allurements,
Swirling,
Silky,
Swirling,
To benefit from temporary exposures,
A bare act
Performed for feet,
Tickled by staring at windows.

71. Breathe

Just breathe;
Let them watch you breathe.
Don't wait for the cold to capture your bones;
Don't wait for the summer sunshine to melt your
emotions.
Take over the battle and let them see
Not your victory.
Just let them watch you breathe.

Let the flowers hide beneath the ashes;
Let the green grass dry while waiting for the sunset.
Take over the revolution and let them see
Not your reality.
Just let them watch you breathe.

Let not the love quotes swing in the air alone;
Let not the love songs moan alone.
Take over the prejudices and let them see
Not your mysteries.
Just let them watch you breathe.

Breathe. Breathe. Breathe.
The world you dream of is not far.
Let your fears calm down;
Let all punishments be borne.
Let them see

Not your gemstone crown.
Just let them watch you breathe.
Shhh . . .
Breathe.

72. That Awkward Moment

Half-woven friendships,
That stood against the world
Once upon a time,
With one happily ever after,
Have now reunited
Again
To kindle back the lost moments.
Such silence has been established,
Awkwardness beyond measure.
Still,
Both ends hope to meet
On the same platform,
Ignoring the obvious breaks,
Still quietly questioning
When had the other been.

Untimely phone calls
Ringing endlessly
On silent mode,
Waiting to be picked up,
Innocently and randomly
Validating the statement
About friendships
That was written out of experience.

73. Methods of Her Existence

Silk curtains
Waving to the windows
Placed on the second side of the road
Behave like teenagers
Lost in their first love,
Covering shadows and shades,
Mingling with the gentle breeze,
Giggling and laughing,
As if burying mystic moments,
Not paying attention to the loneliness of the walls,
Those fail to protect
The destined love.

What is meant to happen will happen
In one way or the other.
No force has ever succeeded in diverting
Fate
Of the gold silver diamonds
As they will land
Today
Or tomorrow
On the bodies that were ordered to carry them.

74. Branches Be in Between

Impressions by the evening shadows
Lit up the dreams held hostage by the sky,
Revealing golden speeches
And dragging dazzling intelligence hand in hand,
Gracefully bowed to the words hanging high.

Dark disappointments of the occasion
Sympathize with enigmatic silence,
Symbolizing the flowers in a bouquet
That is always arranged to perfection,
Leaving enough place
To let one thorn highlight its presence,
Surrounded by everything beautiful,
Like running parallel with the dimensions
Of today's world.
Oh, so influential!

Like branches placed parallel with creativity
Of obsessive perseverance,
Oh, so inspirational!

75. Delicate Dynasties

Seconds of surrealism,
Ticking in slow motion,
Speak,
One is always incomplete without the other;
Such is the philosophy placed in ragged textures.

Secrets, once again,
Find their way back to her,
Whispering about revolutions,
Evolutions,
All hypothetical inventions
In favor of mankind—
An origin of double-faced questions.

Scheduling a meeting with wintry December
That shall last long enough to define short-lived
momentums,
Providing logic,
To reprint her resolutions,
Only this time,
They would be framed,
Properly measured to fit the poles,
Supporting communications
With whatever reality is left for her,
For whatever remains now
Had never really owned her,
But hope is such a thing,
Which wants her to believe
That lies are much better to be with,

And with whatever fantasy is left of her,
She chooses to walk away and finally greet her soul.

Power comes to those who have the power to choose
between nurturing the delicate and giving birth to a
dynasty.

76. Hustle and Bustle

Smoothly sinking in the snowflakes,
Taking a stroll,
Accompanied by the streetlights,
Drumbeats,
Exploding to match with the flickering heights
Of drowning respects,
Flying high,
Flying high,
In search of isolated lands,
Compassed with linking waters,
Flowing like a rhythmic—
So divine.

Spraying paints on rebellious attitudes,
Shading faces,
Stopping fading phases,
Attempting to redefine ethics,
Passed on from generations,
Walking behind.

Mixed and combined cultures
Collide with the performances
Decorated by laces and anchors,
Elegantly
Walk on the stage of shame
Constructed to carve
The shape of
The one and only rebel.

77. That's a Typo

T y p e
T i c k
T y p e
T y p e

Flip-flop letters
Engraved in classic books
Distract the youth and the old,
Adding glares and stares
To the elements of thinking,
Ready to explode into a bubble
With sounds of silence,
While cats walking on the road,
Sticks scattered into pieces;
Each word above
Only explains one thing—
Nothing can be achieved when surrounded by
hypocritical sanity,
Unless everything is viewed with sane propensity.

Quotes occupying the gaps in quotation marks
Ensure
The desperation of every breathing heart
To stand apart
From the noisiness of the crowd
And conquer—the quest that requires refreshments.
Repeat,
Repeat,
Don't conquer yet.

Wait

For autumn to settle on the ground,

For winter to find its way through the whistling ground,

For summer to rest its arrows and bows on lean shoulders,

For love to be set free and find its way back to you.

78. Sipping Digital Kisses

Entering the café,
From a distance,
She noticed
The buzzing of the disconnected minds didn't stop,
Even after searching on tables,
Pushing chairs,
Smiling at strangers,
Hoping for some sensible conversations.
Finally, she settled at a corner
In the center of the ambience
Highlighted by the awkwardness
And expressions,
Placing the gift
In the center,
Removed from the bag
And kept it open for anyone to steal.

A performance for which
Only her lonely hands applauded for so many years,
Courage for which only her conscience praised for so
many years.
Men who still held the power to judge by appearances
Were defeated today
By a pretty face,
Which wasn't covered by any shades of red.

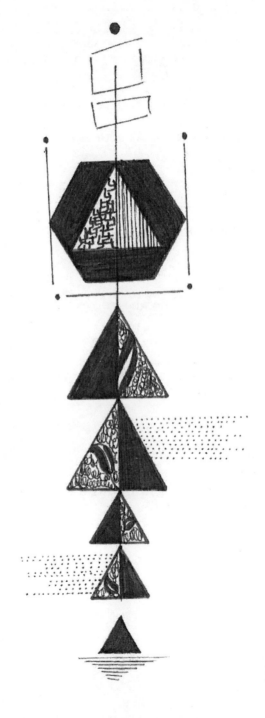

79. Fairy Tale Sweet

Fictional characters speak with me,
Like telling a story
Repeatedly—
No morals,
No values,
Just him and me.

Like how the midnight moment
Brings reality
Into the lives of those who believe,
Erasing every faith
And yet challenging the fantasy
To take the soulful heart
Into a world full of "Till death do us part."

Personalities,
Which talk to me
About the endings—happy and silly,
Questioning the systems of how
Processes are made to distinguish two meaningful
existences.

80. Methods of Existing

A time where every other creation is dealing
With the challenges of the end of believing in something
real,
A wave of realization brushed through the struggling
hearts,
Soothing the knots of misery,
Softening the fluctuating doubts,
Giving them strength and time to pause,
Relive the exact experiences of confusion,
Shift the seats, and take the chance to explain
To their own other self,
For each time a good shade would attempt
To smudge the grounds of fundamental rights.
It has never stopped to hunt for dark sides.
Now is the second.
The list of numbers is torn
To ashes,
From which a new soul will arrive
And teach the world to survive with a shine.

81. Pink Socks

A blink
Is all that it takes
To let go,
Let go
Of the pieces we hold
So tight
And listen to them fall on the ground,
Watch them turn into ashes.

Like a guardian,
You make sure
Every element is scattered,
Distant enough
Not to find its way back
To the gaps and cracks
Left open by her.

A mother nurturing the truth,
A father wandering like a fool,
What is left to earn
But the pink socks kept in the store?

Closets,
Closets,
Floating on the surface of memories,
Show manifestation of her forgotten beliefs.

Black,
Black
Are her footprints now,

Leaving small fragments
And packing the rest
With every step.

Like a guardian,
Make sure
Every element is scattered,
Distant enough
Not to find its way back
To the pink socks
Being mirrored on the closet,
Hanging in the black store.

82. Shutters

shutters,
shutters,
pull down the shutters.
don't let them see the things
which don't matter,
like the stupid boy who walks on the road with his
broken bike,
like the hopeless mother who is searching for her
daughter
at midnight.
in the middle of the night,
when the world is blind,
open the window and let them step inside
to capture the struggle of the poor who sneak in through
the cracks on the floor,
to confide in those who never blinked twice
and missed a laughing sight.
the clock tickles again,
left,
right,
left,
right,
and the pendulum finally quits being punctual all the
time,
breaks all the strings,
and sleeps elegantly
on the lap of the wooden floors
illuminated bright,
so bright!

83. Happy Dates

Sweet gifts,
Surprises
By persistent efforts,
Leading to consistent trials and errors.

Pleasing the self with materialistic beings,
Resorts,
Places,
Safe harbors of the lonely travelers,
Meeting at the same time,
Different places,
Different resorts,
Meaning the same names,
Zones carrying time,
Reaching out to those who
Sleep quiet.

Typing poetry
In a digitalized symmetry,
Circling around the lifestyles
Of those who want to revolutionize
Traditional natures
Of mountains and the seas,
Is the outdated idea
Of you and I,
You and I
Coordinating deadlines,
Starting by every breath we take,
Some hastily,
Some completely.

Distributing surprises
And sweet gifts
Consistently to the lonely travelers
Who will eventually sleep quiet.

84. Secluded Shelves

Crashing the shelves sideways,
Turning back and analyzing the damage,
How much good is good enough?
How much good isn't good enough?

Gathering fragments of misplaced words
Fallen on the carpet,
Playing the game of guessing who is responsible,
"Not me,
Not me,"
She whispers,
Like a prayer.

Footsteps approaching near,
Her scars
Somehow
Own the power
To intimidate her yearlong effort,
So suffice the trend of desperation.

Slowly,
Witnessing the layers of his power,
She stands up,
Tumbling,
But steady and tall,
Inviting the socially acclaimed mind-sets
To defeat her now.
Last chance,
Last chance!

Mysterious morals written on the shelves
Hide with fear—a conclusion for ignominy,
Staring at the raging emotions
That were being shared by their territories.

85. Predictions

She will be watching you write your perfect story,
Drinking clearly,
Smoking mischievously,
Blowing whistles,
Taking the streets for granted
That they will stand still and turn when you command
them.
Every corner
Has your darkest thought stored,
And when the structures fall,
Shattering pieces will fly,
Blending the wind along,
Bending the fate along,
The scripts of the spells
Pronounced by her eyes.

A new world will rise,
Submerging the imprudence of its ancestors,
Framing one rule,
Dictating
Simple rules
To every hand
Manipulated and compromised,
Teaching them loyalty,
Paying them royalty
For standing quiet
With fingers on their lips.

86. Forged Signatures

Background tones,
Mismatching,
Mismatching;
Tapping feet,
Sarcastic,
Sarcastic.

Stitching loose threads of her wedding dress,
Trying to forget the time,
Walking past the cornfields,
Misty hopes surrounding her courage,
Searching for lost pieces of her rings,
Only to carve them back,
Leaving sufficient gaps in between
To accommodate her mistakes,
Regrets, and lessons.

Embossed on the walls
Are her theories about people,
Reading each day,
From a different angle,
Only to remember them in different shades.

Replacing every piece with shapeless boxes,
An act,
A behavior,
Like childlike anger,
Like a lover's hopeless wish,

She ends her day with lights turned on
And twitches the switches,
Waiting,
Waiting for him to come and turn them off.

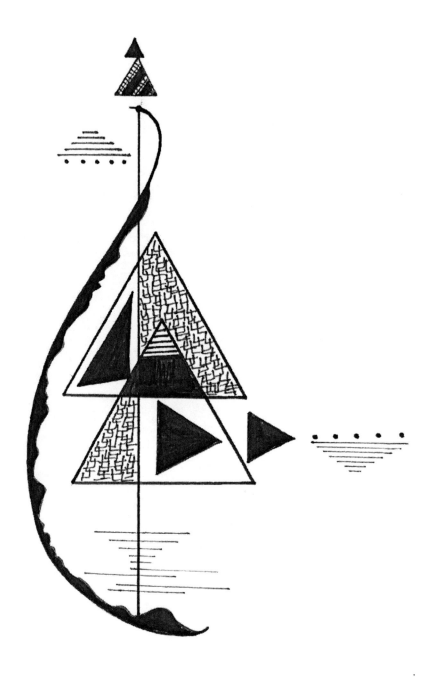

87. Scripted Innocence

The only truth that ever shows its presence
Is when the cold wind embraces your face,
Asking you to let go of everything comfortable,
Asking you to forgive everything miserable.

Acting contradictory,
Trading places with ceaselessly crazy,
Requesting the night to simply stand beside
And watch love emerge from the haze,
The dust of shame,
And fear of their names.
She stepped out,
Forgetting the curves,
Perfecting the lines,
Touching his heart,
Breathing his calmness inside,
Unleashing every pride,
Every curse
Just one last time,
For no one else had ever justified
Having the face of love.
They touched the impossible
One last time,
Because
If one was visible,
The other was in denial,

Rejecting the fate of love.
They swirled gracefully
In circles,
Completing the balance of life.

88. Intentional Divisions

A feeling is sinking in.
What if there's no one to hold on to?
What if there's no melody to smoothen the waves?

There will always be an alternative
To the reality,
Which will be sweeter than an optimistic fantasy,
Challenging every motive of the souls that pretend
To exist
Amidst the pretentious youth
That is craving for spaces
Empty enough for their silent screams to echo,
Like a daze,
Like a trip,
And dragging the voices along the shores
Of empty dreams,
Deficient,
The deficient,
Will never interfere with what's composed by the
universe
But act as a substitute to an alternative destiny.

A disgraceful ordeal for the insensible personalities and
disciplined hearts.

89. Shadows and Trees

Crawling under the bed of the fallen,
Who lay so still and strong,
Waiting to be punished for protecting
The world where fools belonged,
She carried your gift of love,
Waiting to sell along the streets
Of shadows and trees
That covered the dreams above
With lights shooting erratically,
A dream,
A dream
Imitating the fantasies
Of those who lay so still and strong,
Waiting to be punished for protecting her love.

Crawling under the bed of the fallen,
She carried the mistakes
With such grace,
Swirling and turning;
She paused for a second and never opened the doors
To her world again.

90. Found My Way Back Home

Letting go,
Letting go
Will not hold much value
Once you find something new to hold on to.

Run on the white sand of the universe;
Walk on the rhythmic tunes of what life teaches.
Letting go,
Letting go
Will not hold much value
Once you find someone old to hold on to,
Who reminds you of the pieces you were scared to put
together,
Who reminds you that everything around is as beautiful
as you.

Two footsteps will blend into one
Once they will find you and show you the directions
to your home.
It's time to stop traveling in search of green forests,
To get lost and hope to be found
By the invincible.

Only you can find your way back home,
Only you can find your way back home.

91. My Chipped Cup

Avoiding the expressions of her loved ones,
Brewing tea at the counter,
Thinking about questions,
Afraid to face the answers,
Closing her eyes,
Sipping the drink with a smile,
Relieved that nobody will ever watch her so vulnerable,
So happy,
Relieved that nobody will ever watch her so delicate,
So pretty,
And how courageously
She steals her moments with her chipped cup
Just few times a day,
Just few times a day,
She lets the vessel
Absorb her soul and give her back a different version.

With every sip,
She trades a thought
By trading an answer
Just for one more drink!

92. Racing Roads

Father!
Son!
Father!
Son!
Don't win the game,
For it is now my turn to prove
To the roads
On which I made decisions
That you are not my worst mistake
But just a spontaneous one;
If only I hadn't turned away,
If only I hadn't looked away,
You wouldn't be racing with me here.

Roads,
Roads
Turn unpredictable.
Forgive the unforgivable
By handing over the everlasting gift of memories.
Racing with me
Are the racing roads;
Racing with me are the boards.

93. Two Half Barrels

Conveying the truth is half easy,
Half lazy
When the better half is conflicted
While choosing the better version of you.
The truth,
The truth
Is always better when misunderstood,
Giving an excuse to complete
The inevitable fragrance of philosophy,
Blending the two incomplete barrels to roll,
Roll,
And collide into each other to form something total:
A shape,
A color,
A dimension,
A world
Of just the two,
The two,
Just the two.

Tumbling down,
Tumbling down
Are the two half barrels
Competing against each other,
With each other
To touch the finish line,
To taste the end first
And be the one ready,
For a beginning.

94. Million Mistakes

What could possibly be the right word
To renew the strength that has been sleeping
For a long time?
Sentences that have been loosely tied to one another,
Falling apart,
To bring together the reincarnated
Concepts of love and misery,
To speak to every generation
With kindness
Yet with a disconnected mentality
Only to speak in a language of the naive,
To interpret the tangible and the intangible
With methods rhyming with the rhythm
Of sanity
And smoothly
Move through the transition of deliberation and
desperation,
To meet the final chapter of destiny,
A satisfying lesson to be learned
Amongst the insane spellings of vulnerability and
delicacy.
Such precedence!
Such amusement
Of the gaps left open between generations,
Between three generations!

95. Smoking on the Pavement

Shoes that walk on the warm pavements
In summer
With laces open,
Wanting to pretend that they carry an attitude,
To be courageous,
To be rebellious
And struggle to survive in the aura of what is right,
Who knows what is right,
Who feels what is right
Are the ones to rebel against the invisible right,
Are the ones to struggle through the night,
With the universe conspiring against the history,
Contradicting the irony of manipulation,
Debating with the metaphors of reality,
Smoking the vapor on the pavement,
A division of the traffic of life
And a peaceful walk of life,
Both possessing an intensity
Of resurrection
Through one another,
With subtle disparity
Speaking the moral of the story,
And the moral of the story will be,
Could be,
Should be to inhale the pure air of one hemisphere
And exhale the air to a second hemisphere.

96. Ninety-Six

Knitting sweaters on the comfortable couch,
Stitching threads on a secondhand machine
Are the worn-out hands,
Tired hands
That hold together the stories of children and betraying
men together,
Weaving a book
Filled with insane fantasies,
Leading an example of failed relationships
When the whole world is talking about
Little heartbreaks and many disappointments,
And still hoping to stand out amongst the crowd
Of typical endings,
Reciting grandmother's values,
Dejecting grandfather's morals,
Laying down a pattern of contradiction
Of men and women,
Trying to pamper the children—newborn—
And knit a shield of protection
Against the unforgiving world of lost,
Only to create a world for the found,
For the found,
For the found
An everlasting world for the ones who can easily be
convinced
And not be adulterated
By the mistakes of the others
For the rest of their lifetime,
For the rest of their lifetime!

97. Ninety-Seven

Whiskey liquids that melt on the skin
Of ladies so curious,
Like cats,
Like cats
Digging out the lands,
Carving out the sands,
So wet,
So wet,
Building castles with fragmented sand,
Falling apart
With just the power of a blowing sand,
Which will take away all the hard work
Of a child who believes in constructive dreams,
Dominating the supervisory commands of authority,
Proving them with dictating reality
To live life with simplicity,
With simplicity!

Simple alphabets, in the end, hold the power to destroy
the manipulated dreams and give a chance to realistic
dreams.

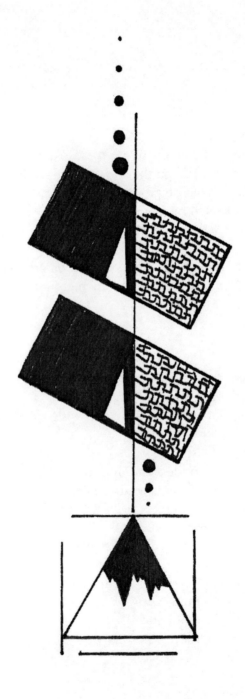

98. Ninety-Eight

Age-old mascaras
Smudging through the blinks of wasted eyes
Trying to see through the eyes of failed lands,
Not able to establish grounds of principles,
With tormented memories,
Still,
Still
Running through the mesh of common grounds,
Frustrated not to find the common grounds
Of likes,
Dislikes,
Mathematics,
Statistics,
Graphics,
And methodic.
Searching for the souls possessed with a true heart is
never a stop
For a forever
To come to an understanding with
A side that has never been successful
In being understood
By even the most intellectual
Or by even the most foolishly productive men of the
generations
Who have been carving structures of cement,
Concrete with mud,
Solid with the thoughts
Of those who lost to win a battle,

With the ones who lost a fight with the ones who won,
Irrespective of the sentences,
Irrespective of the words,
From the lost plans!

99. The Last Letter

Afternoon heat,
Midday summer heat,
Burn the café stops,
Lick the unspoken kisses goodbye,
Bring together happy lost souls
To explore a beautiful day,
To explore an unplanned night,
Feeling shy,
Feeling shy,
Turning away,
Hiding the overwhelming expressions
From each other,
Hiding the vulnerable shades of their souls.
Explode,
Explode
Into a bubble of unpredictable
Love,
Lust,
Shame,
Renaming the game
To replay
Again and again,
Setting a concept for
Writing a last letter
To each other,
One that will fly to the other side,
Tangled in the air,
Caught up in the net of climatic changes,
But will finally arrive
At a destination where it was meant to be.
Surprisingly,

It feels a familiar touch when the hands unfold the page.
Oh, it's him!
Oh, it's her!
This is destiny.
So keep believing in what you want;
What is yours will always find its way back to you!
It always does!